# SERGEI RACHMANINOFF

# PRELUDE, Opus 3, No. 2 in C-sharp Minor

# TEN PRELUDES, Opus 23

Piano Solo

EDITED BY
RUTH LAREDO

*Recording: The Complete Works of Rachmaninoff*
*CBS Masterworks—79700 (7 Record Set)*
*Ruth Laredo, Pianist*

# C.F. PETERS CORPORATION
## NEW YORK LONDON FRANKFURT

# PREFACE

Shortly after my last recording session at CBS of the complete Rachmaninoff solo piano works, C.F. Peters Corporation invited me to begin yet another project — to edit the complete Rachmaninoff Preludes in a new performing edition. I felt very enthusiastic about the idea, and could hardly wait to begin.

For a start, I would have to locate the original manuscripts and then determine what changes would be necessary for an edition suitable for the 1980's.

I soon discovered that this was not an easy task. Although the manuscripts of the *Preludes Opus 23* and *Opus 32* are listed as items in the State Central Glinka Museum of Musical Culture in Moscow, my personal requests for information about the documents went unanswered. After many months of silence from the Soviet Union, Don Leavitt, a friend who also happens to be Chief of the Music Division of the Library of Congress, drafted a letter on my behalf in an attempt to obtain information and photocopies of the Preludes.

The reply, when it finally came, was terribly ambiguous and downright discouraging. According to the curator of the Museum, the Rachmaninoff Preludes were either "missing" or "unavailable." By then, it became apparent that I could not expect cooperation from the Glinka Museum of Musical Culture.

Therefore, I had to turn to other sources. Mrs. Natalia Rachmaninoff had made a generous gift of her husband's original scores to the Library of Congress in Washington, D.C. I was permitted to study the originals and to obtain photocopies at my discretion. In addition, thanks again to Don Leavitt, I discovered an unusual two-piano score of the famous *C-sharp Minor Prelude* which eventually became the model for my work on all of the Preludes.

During the arduous preparations for recording all of Rachmaninoff's solo works, I grew to feel very close to this austere man whose music expressed such rich melancholy. The years of playing his music gave me a strong instinct about the man himself, so that when I began to pore through the Gutheil edition of the *Preludes Opus 23,* I knew they had to have been altered by someone else.

Contrasting the first edition of *Opus 23* (printed in Moscow by Gutheil in 1903) with the manuscript copy of the *C-sharp Minor Prelude,* I knew that my instincts about Rachmaninoff had to be correct. Rachmaninoff's own compositional style was clear, exact, simple and unadorned. The Gutheil (with no editor named) was a mass of inconsistent, unnecessary and largely misleading dynamics, tempo markings and phrasings. Someone had tampered with Rachmaninoff's score, adding his own very personal (though anonymous) interpretation of Rachmaninoff's intentions. This was common practice in 1903. Today we are accustomed to the Urtext, the original; to what the composer had in mind.

In that spirit, I decided to use the recorded performances of Rachmaninoff himself to help form the basis of this edition. With the manuscript copies of the *C-sharp Minor Prelude* and the *Corelli Variations* as a guide, I have tried to allow the music of the Preludes themselves to shine through. I've given some dynamic and tempo indications, but I've totally eliminated the clutter of extraneous markings.

For the student, I've indicated my own fingerings, which I hope will be of help in this very difficult music and, finally, I have tried to illuminate the work of this great creator of incomparable beauty and sentiment in an edition for a new generation of pianists to discover and enjoy.

RUTH LAREDO

# NOTE TO STUDENTS

Sergei Rachmaninoff was not only one of the greatest pianists who ever lived, but a distinguished conductor and prolific composer as well. His piano writing exacts tremendous demands upon the pianist, extending the limits of the piano's resources, reaching beyond Chopin, Liszt and Brahms, to an orchestral sonority unparalleled in the literature. My own personal experience with this very difficult and richly textured music has taught me a great deal about the piano and what it can do.

The technical challenge is sometimes awesome. One must have courage, dedication and patience to attempt this music. It is virtually an orchestral text written for one person with only two hands. Rachmaninoff's ardent romanticism and his equally strong reticence as a human being make the interpretation of his music even more complex than one would expect at first.

The performance of music is a living thing, almost impossible to describe, but I have gained enormous insight from my experience with Rachmaninoff. It is my hope that others will find his music as genuinely rewarding as I have.

— R.L.

## Prelude Opus 3, No. 2 in C-sharp Minor

When Rachmaninoff was nineteen and fresh out of the Moscow Conservatory, he published a set of five pieces as Opus 3. The second piece in this set, *Prelude in C-sharp Minor,* became an immediate sensation, and established the young composer's reputation all over the world.

Because he failed to secure an international copyright, Rachmaninoff received only forty rubles (or about twenty dollars!) for his work. The Prelude was printed in many countries, enjoying enormous success under such titles as "Judgment Day" and "The Burning of Moscow." It was so popular that it led to Rachmaninoff's first concert tour of America.

Ultimately, the Prelude became a burden for Rachmaninoff, whose name grew to be synonymous with the piece. No matter what he played or where he played, Rachmaninoff's public demanded the famous Prelude and would not let him leave the stage until he had played it as an encore.

As a piece of music, the *C-sharp Minor Prelude* has a characteristically Russian flavor. It begins and ends with the sound of bells which Rachmaninoff loved so dearly all his life. The Prelude requires physical strength, clarity, and a good sustaining *legato.* The massive chords must give a sense of dynamic movement as the harmonies change. The middle section, marked *Molto allegro e agitato,* builds gradually in dynamics and in tempo to a climax marked *Prestissimo.*

The tremendous recapitulation, written on three staves, requires concentration and power. Listen to those chords — let their sounds ring out like the bells in a cathedral!

This edition incorporates all of what I believe to be Rachmaninoff's authentic tempo markings and musical directions. Unlike other editions, whose dynamics range all the way from *ppp* to *sffff,* Rachmaninoff's manuscript is far more conservative. His own tempo markings and phrasings speak for themselves — allowing the piece to appear for the first time in print as he really intended it.

**Prelude Opus 23, No. 1 in F-sharp Minor**

This Prelude should be played songfully and with an expressive *legato*. I've indicated fingerings to enable both hands to remain as quiet as possible — staying on the keys with very little extraneous motion.

The left hand has a free-flowing melodic line which should sing in contrast to the right hand's longer sustaining voice. The tempo marking is an approximate indication and can vary. This Prelude should ebb and flow like the tide — never metronomic.

Although I've indicated *tenuto* marks on some left hand melodic notes, they are not to be accented. They are notes to be 'leaned' on. This piece does not have sharp edges, but it broadens enormously in sound and expression at the climax.

**Prelude Opus 23, No. 2 in B-flat Major**

This Prelude is excellent for building strength in the left hand. It is a heroic piece of virtuosity, similar to many of the Chopin Etudes and Preludes.

The left hand pattern, once comfortably established, becomes easier and can greatly help to strengthen left hand articulation. Though reminiscent of Chopin's *Prelude Opus 28, No. 3 in G Major,* where the left hand figuration floats independently of the right hand melody, this Rachmaninoff Prelude is on a much grander dynamic scale.

Use little or no pedal when practicing this Prelude. Played strictly as a study, it can highlight just what the fingers are truly achieving. Wonderful results can be gained from working patiently on the Prelude — such as improved clarity in the left hand and increased strength in both hands.

**Prelude Opus 23, No. 3 in D Minor**

These fingerings may seem unorthodox, but the aim is to achieve independence of each finger. Do not rely on the pedal to sustain long lines. In fact, it would be beneficial to practice this prelude entirely without pedal at first in order to hear both hands accurately. Pedal can be added later on for color — not to produce *legato*.

Dots indicate lightness of touch rather than a short *staccato*. This prelude has a rather whimsical, Tchaikovsky-like flavor. The *Tempo di minuetto* marking adds to this impression.

**Prelude Opus 23, No. 4 in D Major**

Due to the large leaps in this prelude, the hands must be relaxed in order to avoid strain. Relax and stretch comfortably, giving both hands the freedom to sustain the wide melodic lines with a good healthy *legato*.

Do not break the line by changing hand positions unless absolutely necessary. Shift wherever possible, changing fingers silently over the same note rather than lifting the hands from the keys. The fingerings are indicated with this smoothness in mind.

The right hand must sing as if it were a human voice — accompanied by a cello in the left hand. Both hands should convey a rich, singing tone throughout.

**Prelude Opus 23, No. 5 in G Minor**

One of the most familiar of all the Rachmaninoff Preludes, this is also one of the most difficult to play. The rhythm must be solid and dance-like. There is a lilt to this March in a minor key.

A true *staccato* of repeated notes at this tempo is almost impossible. I prefer the idea of space between the notes — a variety of lightness of touch, rather than just a *staccato*. For this reason, I've omitted most of the dots which appear in other versions.

It is almost impossible to achieve muscular relaxation, but too much tension is to be avoided. Stop if it hurts! Work slowly and observe the hands in slow motion to facilitate economy of motion.

The *legato* middle section is a welcome contrast to the repetitive short notes of the March. It helps to relax the hands as well. Try for a dark, rich sound in the low octaves. Build your strength gradually — it will not come overnight.

**Prelude Opus 23, No. 6 in E-flat Major**

Again, Rachmaninoff has written a duet between the upper and lower voices. The right hand needs flexibility and independence from the left in order to sing this lovely melody freely — just as a singer needs a flexible and attentive accompaniment.

Sometimes there can be no fully comfortable fingering, but the *legato* must be continuous in any case. Practice each hand independently, and know the left hand so well that it becomes second nature when added to the right hand.

The beautifully expressive left hand *obbligato* should flow easily and without accent. The piece is an endless melodic line.

**Prelude Opus 23, No. 7 in C Minor**

This is an example of Rachmaninoff's orchestral piano writing. Several textures are in motion at once — the singing upper melody, the somber bass notes, and the light sixteenth note strands spinning their way from one hand to the other. Be sure you know each voice and where it fits into the whole. To produce several kinds of piano sonority all at the same time is not easy, but this is what the piece requires.

**Prelude Opus 23, No. 8 in A-flat Major**

Again, Rachmaninoff creates a beautiful orchestral texture requiring a variety of sonorities, colors and different pianistic touches. The melody in the left hand is *dolce legato* while the sixteenth notes weave about it in the right hand. *Legato,* as alway, is imperative with a light filigreed touch for the right hand and many gradations of sound in between. The long lines and largeness of scope are typical of Rachmaninoff.

The ending is epigrammatic — it speaks like a voice. The last line is similar in feeling to the ending of Chopin's *Impromptu Opus 29, No. 1.* Is it a coincidence that this piece is also in A-flat Major?

**Prelude Opus 23, No. 9 in E-flat Minor**

This piece is as close to an étude as a prelude can be. It is a technical *tour de force* — just as most of the Chopin Etudes are. It must be studied as patiently and methodically as an étude and practiced slowly and carefully until the impossible begins to feel normal. One should try to attain a certain amount of relaxation in the hands while playing this piece, or all will be lost.

Keep a singing *legato* line in the left hand. The source of struggle is in the right hand. Much can be gained by working on such a demanding piece. The fingerings I have indicated are intended to give the right hand the freedom and control necessary for such extended passage work.

There is some lovely music to be found despite the technical struggle. It is well worth the effort.

**Prelude Opus 23, No. 10 in F-sharp Major**

This Prelude is reminiscent of the Chopin *Etude Opus 25, No. 7 in G-sharp Minor,* perhaps because of the singing bass line with the expressive right hand accompaniment. Although Rachmaninoff's Prelude is in a major key, there is a somberness about it, like the smile on an unhappy man's face. There is an intimacy about this prelude unlike any of the others.

The right hand stays close to the keys while the left hand sings. There is relatively little motion involved in either hand. As the piece expands, the sounds grow in intensity and there are more leaps, more distance to travel over the keys, but all of this comes to a tranquil, introspective close. Emotionally similar to the last movement of Robert Schumann's *Scenes from Childhood,* it is a poetic comment on what has gone before — very introspective and beautiful.

— R.L.

*A Monsieur A. Arensky*

# PRELUDE

Edited by Ruth Laredo

S. Rachmaninoff, Op. 3, No. 2

Edition Peters 66900

# TEN PRELUDES, OPUS 23
## I.

Edited by Ruth Laredo

S. Rachmaninoff, Op. 23, No. 1

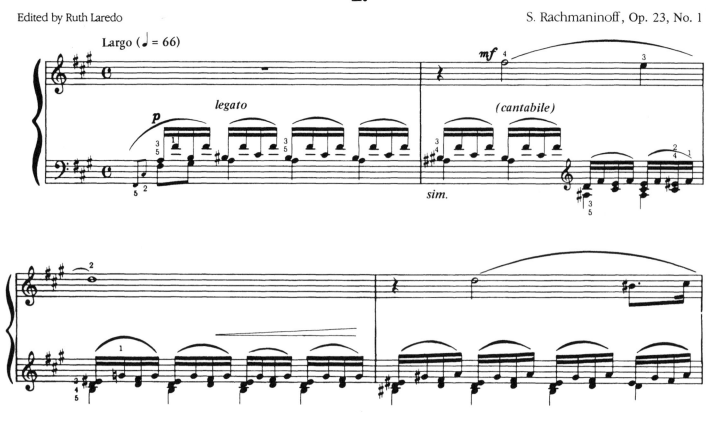

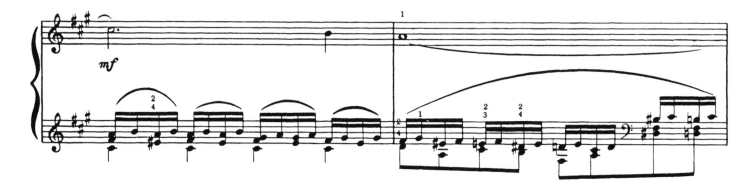

**Edition Peters 66900**

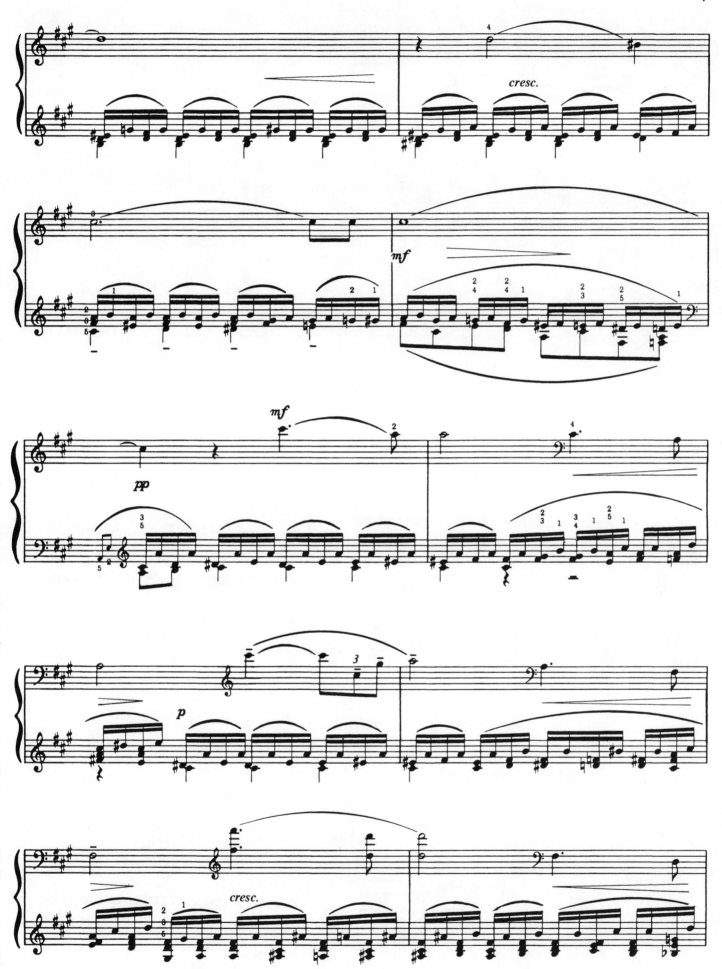

# II.

S. Rachmaninoff, Op. 23, No. 2

# III.

S. Rachmaninoff, Op. 23, No. 3

Tempo di minuetto (♩=80)

# IV.

S. Rachmaninoff, Op. 23, No. 4

# V.

S. Rachmaninoff, Op. 23, No. 5

Alla marcia (♩=112)

Un poco meno mosso

Tempo I

# VI.

S. Rachmaninoff, Op. 23, No. 6

# VII.

S. Rachmaninoff, Op. 23, No. 7

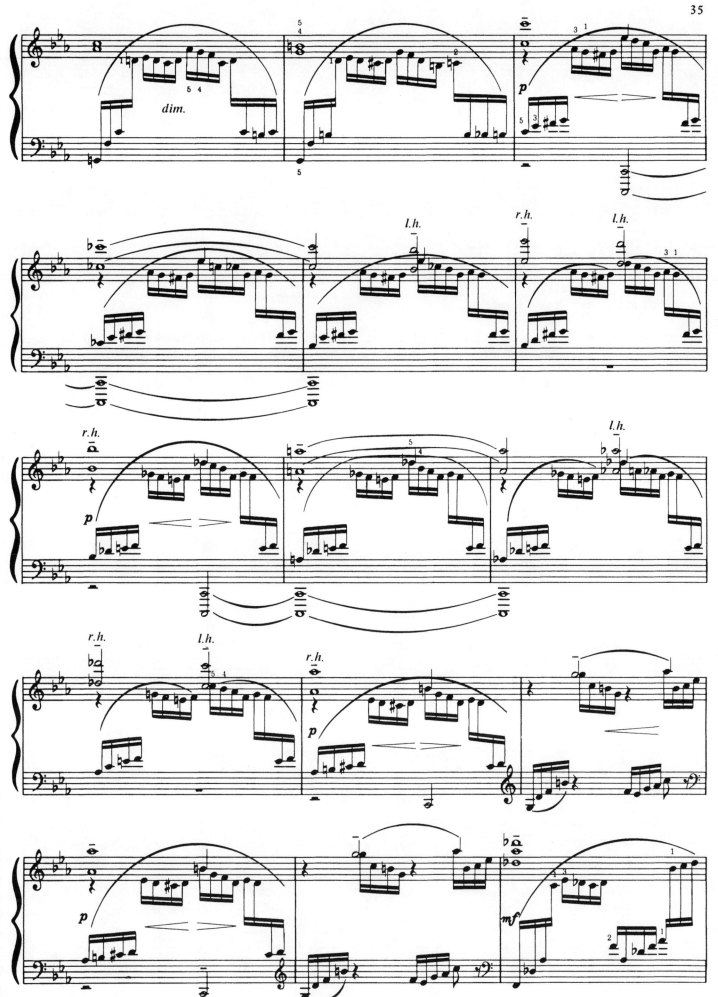

# VIII.

S. Rachmaninoff, Op. 23, No. 8

Allegro vivace (♩=160)

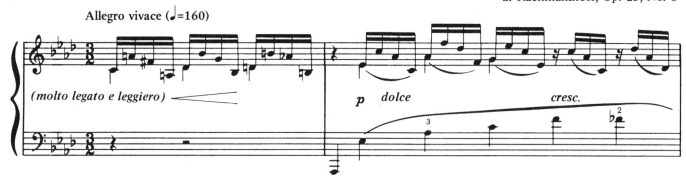

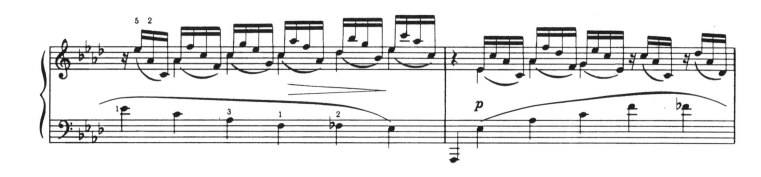

# IX.

S. Rachmaninoff, Op. 23, No. 9

**Presto** ( ♩ = 126)

# X.

**Largo** (♩ = 58) *(molto legato e espressivo)*